SLAPPY

Once there was a little called Slappy. He had nice big which came down with a slip-slap when he walked. And that, as you may guess, was why he was called . Now did not want to be a duck. He wanted to be a person, but don't ask me why!

 didn't want to practise

his quacking lesson, and he
didn't want to go with his
two to take his
lesson, and he didn't want
to do anything that a well-
mannered duck should do.

"I don't want to be a
duck," said . "I want
to be a PUSSON and see
the great wide ."
"It's pronounced PERSON,"

said his , but  did not listen. He just moped around and got thinner and

sadder until his  said,

"All right then! Go out and

see the  ."

 slip-slapped around

the stuffing his clothes

into a spotted  . He

gave his  a peck as a

kiss and said goodbye to

his . They went off

to their quacking teacher

in their pretty quacking

lesson 🎩 but 🦆 went

up over the hill to the

great wide 🌍.

🦆 marched along gaily,

singing a silly little song.

Suddenly he looked over a

stone 🧱 and saw a 👨‍🌾

hoeing 🥕. Using his best

manners, 🦆 asked, "Will you

kindly tell me where the

great wide 🌍 is, and how

I can become a PUSSON?"

The  only shouted,

"SHOO!" felt sad, but

he went slap-slapping along

the ∕, and pretty soon he

saw a little brown 🏠 with a

fat 👩 in the yard. She

was hanging 👕s and 👖

on the line.

🦆 said politely, "Would

you please tell me, Your

Gracious Majesty, how I can

become a pusson like you?"

"Why, you see, you just have

to learn to carry a ," said the , putting it right on Slappy's back. struggled and humped, and over went the upside down in the dirt. The scolded and chased him until she was out of breath. kept running until he saw a resting under a . "Please," said ,

"would you tell me how I
can become a pusson and see

the great wide ?"

"First," said the  "you
have to carry a  if you
want to be a person."

He passed his to ,
but it was too heavy. It fell
on almost as hard as
the 's .

"Thank you," said as he
got up and rubbed his .

He went along until he

met a school  coming down

the  with her  in a  .

"Good morning," said the and replied, "Good

morning!"

"Would you tell me where the

great wide is, and how

I can become a pusson?"

"Say PERSON," said the

. was quite dis-

couraged, for he knew he

could never learn to say

person. He said "Good-day,"

to the  and went down the until he saw an  painting a picture.

"May I ask," said 🦆 speaking politely, "how can I become a pusson?"

"Your shape is wrong," said the 👨‍🎨. "You'll have to be stretched out and jammed in and flattened down."

So he stretched 🐥's 🦶🦶, and flattened his 🔥 and was

just going to jam in his

when gave a great jump

and ran away. "Thank you

kindly," he said and he

turned and started back down the past the with the , past the with the , then past the with the and past the with the . He ran up the long and over the out of the great wide into his own where he fell into a corner.

His came and saw him.